THE FROG THAT CROAKED

by -

Tutu Mele

Copyright 2015 by Mary Martin
Aka- Tutu Mele
ISBN Createspace   softcover **ISBN-13: 978-1517628567**
1517628567

Rev. date: 08/1/2015
The Frog That Croaked

The Frog That Croaked

By –

Tutu Mele

Acknowlegements

This book is dedicated to all boys and girls who are learning about nature. They will love reading about this egg as he turns into a frog. If your child is interested in nature, they will love following this frog as he goes through his changes and leaves his pond and friends and learns to croak.

It is also dedicated to my grandchildren who are just starting school and learning to read. I hope it brings many years of reading pleasure to all preschool and beginning readers. This book fits perfectly into their small hands. Whether your child can read or likes to be read to, he or she will love this book.

Thank you to my good friend and author, Rhonda Feltman, for helping me get my children's books published. Thank you to all the children who are interested in nature and question how and why things go through changes.

THE FROG THAT CROAKED

by -

Tutu Mele

Hi!
I am little and round.
I am in an egg.
Can you find me?

Look at me! I am not an
egg now.
I can swim fast.
I can see.
I can go, go, go!

I can swim.
See me go!
I am so cool!
I can go fast!

I like to play.
Here is Big Fin.
He is fun. He likes to
play with me. We like
to swim and play and
hide.

We met a rock.
He will not move.
We can play with him.
We can hide and play.
He is a good friend.
Where is Big Fin?

We want a new game.
Where can we go?
I can go out of the pond.
Come with me, Big Fin!
Can you come with me?

I have new legs.
They are so big.
I can go up.
I like to hop and go up.
This is fun!

I can hop.
I can swim.
Poor Big Fin. He is so sad.
He can not go out of the pond.
He can not play with me.

I am glad.
I am so cool.
I can hop and swim with
Big Fin.
I can croak. I can croak
and swim with Big Fin!!!

Tutu Mele

Tutu Mele loves to write books for the beginning reader. Her books usually have a scientific or nature theme. She realizes that children are filled with questions and she has written books that answer these questions about the nature children see around them. She does this in an artistic way that catches the imagination of these younger readers. She keeps the vocabulary at the level so that these beginning readers can read and reread these books on their own. These books are sized to fit into young hands beautifully.

She has dedicated this book to her grandchildren who are learning to read and love the excitement of the outdoors. They love hunting for pollywogs and frogs and learning about them. This book is for all the budding naturalists in every family.

Whether your child can read or enjoys being read to, he or she will enjoy this book.

The Frog That Croaked
Vocabulary

the	frog	that	croaked
egg	am	I	frog
find	look	at	me
see	can	swim	go
cool	play	here	big
fin	fun	rock	met
not	new	game	where
will	we	legs	so
up	can	hop	poor
sad	glad	croak	fast
little	round		

This book is part of a nature series.

Other titles by Tutu Mele include:

The Ugly Bug

The Frog That Croaked

Changing Colors

Little Whale Small

The Bike That Ate Dirt

La Motocicleta Que Come Lodo